WHY BE

CONFIRMED?

by
Bishop Michael Evans

*All booklets are published thanks to the
generous support of the members of the
Catholic Truth Society*

CATHOLIC TRUTH SOCIETY
PUBLISHERS TO THE HOLY SEE

CONTENTS

Abbreviation note: References to the *Catechism of the Catholic Church* may also be abbreviated to *CCC*.

'Then the disciples rejoiced when they saw the Lord.
Jesus said to them again:
"Peace be with you.
As the Father has sent me,
so I send you."
When he had said this he breathed on them and said to them:
"Receive the Holy Spirit"' *(John 20:20-22)*

'You will receive power when the Holy Spirit has come
upon you, and you will be my witnesses... to the ends of
the earth' *(Acts 1:8)*

Every baptised person not yet confirmed can and should
receive the sacrament of Confirmation. Since Baptism,
Confirmation and Eucharist form a unity, it follows that
'the faithful are obliged to receive this sacrament at the
appropriate time', for without Confirmation and
Eucharist, Baptism is certainly valid and efficacious, but
Christian initiation remains incomplete. (*Catechism of the
Catholic Church,* n. 1306)

WHY ALL THE FUSS?

Why does the Catholic Church make such a fuss about the Sacrament of Confirmation? Young people, for example, are often asked to go through a long period of preparation before being confirmed. And why does the Church generally expect a bride and groom to be confirmed before getting married? Surely marriage preparation and the wedding itself are more than enough? And why is Confirmation such an important part of being received into full communion with the Catholic Church, especially when a person has already been confirmed as an Anglican or Methodist? Is all this really necessary, particularly as Confirmation often seems to be the sacrament people most easily forget, with little obvious impact on their lives? For some young people, getting confirmed is the 'sacrament of exit', the time when they feel free to opt out of regular involvement in the worship and life of the Church. Do we remember our own Confirmation? How many people celebrate their Confirmation anniversary each year? Is it really something worth celebrating in the first place?

And then there are all those very different opinions about when we should be confirmed. At what age should a young person usually be confirmed? Should Confirmation be immediately after Baptism (in infancy, as in the

Orthodox Church), before making First Holy Communion, at the same celebration as First Communion, or when a young person is becoming a young adult, mature enough to accept the responsibilities involved in receiving the sacrament? Some people, especially liturgy scholars, insist strongly on restoring the ancient order of the Sacraments of Initiation: Baptism, Confirmation, Holy Communion. Others, especially those involved in pastoral work with young people, stress Confirmation as an opportunity for mature commitment and deeper involvement. Can this sacrament really be all that important and vital when Catholic leaders and thinkers cannot agree on such basic questions, and when practice can differ so greatly from one diocese to another?

Some people say that we are not really sure what Confirmation really means anyway! If that is so, then I ask once again, why all the fuss? There is a simple answer: the Catholic Church at the beginning of the twenty-first century has a clear teaching on the Sacrament of Confirmation. This teaching is rooted in the New Testament (especially St Luke in his Gospel and in the Acts of the Apostles), in the great thinkers of the Church throughout the ages, in the official teaching of the Church, and in the rite of Confirmation itself. My limited aim in this booklet is to present that teaching, and to draw out some of the implications for anyone preparing for Confirmation, for their catechists, and for those of us who have already been confirmed, perhaps many years ago. I will leave others to draw conclusions about the best age or stage for being confirmed. Whatever they decide, however, should be rooted first and foremost in a full and proper understanding of the meaning of the sacrament. Liturgical and pastoral considerations are also important when making such decisions, but they come second to the Church's teaching which has developed over the centuries and which continues to grow towards a maturity of understanding.

THE RITE OF CONFIRMATION

What happens when a person is confirmed? Looking at the ceremony itself gives us a good idea of why this sacrament is so important for our Christian life.

By a bishop

Although a priest is sometimes delegated to administer Confirmation, in our Western churches it is usually the bishop who confirms. A bishop is a successor of the apostles and a servant of the unity of the Church. Being confirmed by a bishop is a powerful sign of our connection with the first beginnings of the Church, and of our involvement in a much wider community than our own parish. It also reminds us of something which lies at the very heart of the meaning of Confirmation: our call to share more fully in the Church's apostolic mission to bring the Good News of Jesus to the world.

Ordinarily the sacrament is administered by the bishop so that there will be a more evident relationship to the first pouring forth of the Holy Spirit on Pentecost. After the apostles were filled with the Holy Spirit, they themselves gave the Spirit to the faithful through the laying on of their hands. Thus the reception of the Spirit through the

> ministry of the bishop shows the close bond which joins
> the confirmed to the Church and the mandate to be
> witnesses of Christ among men and women.
> (*Introduction to the Rite of Confirmation.*[1])

Using chrism

Even when a priest confirms, he always uses oil of
chrism, consecrated by a bishop at the special Chrism
Mass during Holy Week. Only a bishop can make chrism.
Chrism is the most sacred oil used by the Church. It is a
perfumed oil, often a mixture of olive oil and balsam, and
signifies the Gift of the Holy Spirit. It is used for the
dedication of the altar and walls of a new church. Each of
us was anointed with chrism at our Baptism: it was a sign
of our unity with Christ himself who is *the* Anointed One,
our anointed priest, prophet and king. Chrism is a priestly
oil; it is used to anoint the head of a newly-ordained
bishop and the hands of a newly-ordained priest. By our
Baptism, we are all members of a consecrated, priestly
people. Chrism is a royal oil, still used today in the
United Kingdom at the coronation of a king or queen. By
our Baptism, we are the royal family of God himself, the
Lord of Lords and King of Kings; there is no greater
royalty than that! And chrism is also a prophetic oil, used
to anoint us to speak for God in the world, and to
proclaim the Good News of Jesus Christ.

Make sure you do not think of the chrism simply as oil.
Just as the bread of the Eucharist,
after the invocation of the Holy Spirit,
is no longer just bread, but the body of Christ,
so the holy chrism after the invocation
is no longer ordinary oil but the grace of Christ,
which through the presence of the Holy Spirit
instills his divinity into us.
(*St Cyril of Jerusalem.*[2])

Accompanied by a sponsor

Sometimes when we join a new club, we have to be sponsored by someone who is already a member. Each candidate for Confirmation is accompanied by a sponsor, a full member of the Church whose role is 'to take care that the person confirmed behaves as a true witness to Christ and faithfully fulfils the duties inherent in this sacrament' (*Code of Canon Law,* n. 892).

Sponsors should be chosen carefully by the candidates and their families. They need to be mature enough for the role, and practising Catholics who have already been confirmed themselves. Generally, a sponsor should be at least aged sixteen (*Code of Canon Law,* canons 893.1 & 874.1). What is most important is that a sponsor is someone who will be a real example of what it means to live the Catholic faith.

Candidates for Confirmation, as for Baptism, fittingly
seek the spiritual help of a sponsor. To emphasise the
unity of the two sacraments, it is appropriate that this
be one of the baptismal godparents. (*CCC*.[3])

During Mass

Young people are usually confirmed during a special
celebration of Mass, either in their parish or in the
cathedral of the diocese. After the Scripture readings and
the homily, the bishop invites the candidates to stand and
to renew their baptismal promises. Then he extends his
hands over them. He asks God the Father to pour the
Holy Spirit upon them, strengthen them with his gifts and
anoint them to be more like Christ, the Son of God. This
is the prayer he says:

All-powerful God, Father of our Lord Jesus Christ,
by water and the Holy Spirit,
you freed your sons and daughters from sin
and gave them new life.
Send your Holy Spirit upon them
to be their helper and guide.
Give them the spirit of wisdom and understanding,
the spirit of right judgement and courage,
the spirit of knowledge and reverence.
Fill them with the spirit of wonder and awe

in your presence.
We ask this through Christ our Lord.

Then each candidate comes forward with their sponsor
for the central moment of the sacrament. The bishop
anoints the candidate by making the sign of the cross
with chrism on the forehead, saying: 'Be sealed with the
Gift of the Holy Spirit.' While this happens, the sponsor
places his or her right hand on the candidate's shoulder.
The bishop and newly confirmed then wish each other
the gift of God's peace. Once all the candidates have
been confirmed, the celebration continues with the
General Intercessions (or Bidding Prayers) and the rest
of Mass as usual. It is a simple but deeply moving ritual.
The Mass ends with a 'Prayer over the People' which
sums up the meaning and implications of the sacrament
of Confirmation:

God our Father,
complete the work you have begun
and keep the gifts of your Holy Spirit
alive in the hearts of your people.
Make them ready to live his Gospel
and eager to do his will.
May they never be ashamed
to proclaim to all the world Christ crucified,
living and reigning for ever and ever.

> The Sacrament of Confirmation is conferred through the
> anointing with chrism on the forehead, which is done by
> the laying-on of the hands, and through the words: *Be
> sealed with the Gift of the Holy Spirit. (Pope Paul VI.[4])*

Five Key Points

From what happens at Confirmation, it is already clear
what lies at the heart of the meaning of this great
sacrament. There are five key points which need to be
held together in any truly Catholic understanding of this
sacrament. Later, I will explore each of these in detail.

1. Confirmation is a sacrament of initiation, a sacrament
of welcome into the mysteries of Christ and his Church.
It is intimately linked with the other two sacraments of
initiation, Baptism and the Eucharist, and we can
understand it properly only if we preserve that link.

2. Confirmation is, however, a distinct sacrament of the
Church, and we must take this distinctness seriously.

3. Confirmation involves a special giving of the Holy Spirit,
the Spirit already fully bestowed at a person's Baptism.

4. At Confirmation, the Holy Spirit seals, strengthens,
confirms and perfects what was already given in Baptism.

This brings about a deeper unity with the Church, and a strengthening and empowering for what that involves.

5. Although there is a deep and inseparable unity with Baptism, something new is given in Confirmation. We can see this as a commissioning by the Risen Christ in his Church for 'official', public witness to the Good News in the world.

Nearly everyone agrees that Confirmation involves a new giving of the Holy Spirit. Those who advocate early Confirmation tend to stress the first and fourth points above. Those who prefer later Confirmation emphasise the second and fifth. It is essential, however, that we hold together all five. When properly understood, we see that they belong together and explain each other.

> Baptism, the Eucharist and the sacrament of Confirmation together constitute 'the sacraments of initiation', whose unity must be safeguarded. It must be explained to the faithful that the reception of the sacrament of Confirmation is necessary for the completion of Baptismal grace. For 'by the sacrament of Confirmation, the baptised are more perfectly bound to the Church and are enriched with a special strength of the Holy Spirit. Hence they are, as true witnesses of Christ, more strictly obliged to spread and defend the faith by word and deed.' (*CCC*.[5])

CONFIRMATION IS A SACRAMENT OF INITIATION

St Luke writes of a special giving of the Holy Spirit to some believers who had already been baptised in the name of Jesus (*Acts* 8:14-17; 19:5-6; cf. *Hebrews* 6:2). He implies they were missing something essential. Later, these texts became important for understanding Confirmation. Apart from this, however, there is little if any evidence in the first 150 years of the Church for a distinct giving of the Holy Spirit to people who had already been baptised. There seems to have been a single rite of initiation, centred on total immersion in the waters of Baptism. This was sometimes accompanied by symbolic actions which drew out and celebrated its meaning. Gradually, two key aspects of initiation were highlighted, with distinct rituals signifying each aspect.

By AD 200, the initiation rites of many Christian communities had two main elements: immersion in water and an additional ritual signifying reception of the Holy Spirit. This ritual varied from place to place: the laying-on of hands, signing the forehead with a dry thumb, pouring of oil, and eventually making the sign of the cross on the forehead with oil. This was performed by the bishop as high priest and chief shepherd of the local church. It was seen as sealing and completing before the community what had been done immediately before in the comparative privacy of the baptismal pool. It was one element in a single rite of initiation, but it acquired more and more the status of a distinct and important moment in that rite.

Eventually in the West this second ritual became separated in time from Baptism. But it was still regarded as an integral part of a process of initiation which begins in Baptism and reaches its climax in full participation in the Eucharist. This is a point we need to remember. Baptism remains incomplete without Confirmation. Confirmation makes no sense apart from Baptism. Baptism, Confirmation and the Eucharist together are the Church's way of entry into the mysteries of God. For adults who have already reached maturity, the three sacraments are celebrated together, usually at the Easter Vigil Mass. For children gradually developing towards maturity, they are spread out over a number of years. As the introduction to the Rite of Confirmation states, 'those who have been baptised continue on the path of Christian initiation through the sacrament of Confirmation.'

The sacraments of initiation may be celebrated with quite a few years between them, but they are still closely linked. This is an important point for anyone preparing for Confirmation. You need to think afresh about the meaning of your Baptism, and also the place of the Eucharist, the Mass in your life.

Firstly, a piece of research for everyone, whether you are preparing for Confirmation or already confirmed long ago. Find out the date of your Baptism. You may have a copy of your certificate somewhere. If not, find out where you were baptised, and ask the parish secretary there to send you a copy of your certificate, or at least to let you know the date of your Baptism. Then make a special point of celebrating your Baptism anniversary every year. This is your spiritual birthday, a good excuse for a party! Families should celebrate Baptism anniversaries together, not just of each child but also of the parents. Make special cards for each other. Give each other a special anniversary gift. Perhaps at a family meal together on the day, light the candle you were given at your Baptism, or a new one if you no longer have the original.

Secondly, think about who you are because of your Baptism. Why was your Baptism so important? On that day, God our Father adopted you as his own beloved daughter or son, and you became a member of God's great royal family. You became united with the Risen Jesus in an extraordinary way, so closely that you are 'in Christ'. You became a member of his Body, the Church, God's royal, priestly, prophetic people. You became a living stone in the temple where God's Holy Spirit dwells. On your Baptism day, you were anointed with the Holy Spirit. Your Baptism was an Easter Day for you, a Day of Resurrection. You were delivered from the death of sin and raised to a new life in Christ. You were made new, re-created, born again. Everything else in your Christian life flows from

MARY SMITH

through Baptism
on 1st September 1990
you became

a beloved daughter of God our Father;

a member of God's great royal family, the Church;

a personal friend, sister and follower of Jesus our Lord;

a sacred dwelling-place for the Holy Spirit.

Celebrate each year who you are
because of your Baptism,
and as St Paul once wrote,

"Live a life worthy of your vocation"

An example of a Baptism Celebration Certificate which could be given to each candidate preparing for Confirmation.

that moment. Every Easter you are invited to renew your
commitment to living out all that your Baptism means.
Confirmation is much more than simply re-affirming your
Baptism, but it is an opportunity to commit yourself
personally to live your Baptismal calling more faithfully.
That is why the Renewal of Baptismal Promises is part of
the Rite of Confirmation. Look at yourself in your spiritual
mirror. See yourself as God sees you, with all the tender
care and forgiving love that he has for you as his daughter
or son. Be proud of who you are because of God's love,
and be proud to profess and live your faith.

Renewal of Baptismal Promises

Bishop: Do you reject Satan and all his works,
                 and all his empty promises?

Candidates: I do.

Bishop: Do you believe in God, the Father
                 almighty, Creator of heaven and earth?

Candidates: I do.

Bishop: Do you believe in Jesus Christ, his only
                 Son, our Lord, who was born of the
                 Virgin Mary, was crucified, died and

---

was buried, rose from the dead and is now seated at the right hand of the Father?

Candidates: I do.

Bishop: Do you believe in the Holy Spirit, the Lord, the giver of life, who came upon the Apostles at Pentecost, and today is given to you sacramentally in Confirmation?

Candidates: I do.

Bishop: Do you believe in the Holy Catholic Church, the Communion of Saints, the forgiveness of sins, the resurrection of the body, and life everlasting?

Candidates: I do.

Bishop: This is our faith. This is the Faith of the Church. We are proud to profess it in Christ Jesus our Lord.

Candidates: Amen

CONFIRMATION IS A DISTINCT SACRAMENT

The Council of Trent in the sixteenth century taught that Confirmation is a true and proper sacrament of the Church. Whatever people may think about the way Confirmation developed in the West, it remains a distinct sacrament, with something of its own to give to the Christian on the path of welcome into Christ and his Church.

What is a Sacrament?

The Risen Lord has promised to be with us always, to the end of time. How can we be in touch today with Jesus Christ, who no longer walks the earth in the same way as he once did? We believe that his invisible presence is made visible and tangible for us through special 'sacramental' signs. A sacrament is far more than simply a signpost pointing towards something greater elsewhere. Each sacrament is an effective sign which makes present what it signifies. Sacraments are 'specific ways in which, by the power of the Holy Spirit, the Risen Jesus makes his saving presence and action effective in our midst.' Because the Lord is present and at work in them, sacraments 'bring into our lives the life-giving action and even the self-giving of Christ himself.' Through sacramental signs,

instituted by Christ himself, we are put 'in touch' with
the saving mystery of Christ here and now. The more
we respond in faith to his presence, the more a
sacrament becomes a truly life-giving encounter with
Jesus himself. This understanding of 'sacrament' - the
invisible presence and action of the Risen Lord made
powerfully present through visible signs - lies at the
heart of our Catholic faith. (*Catholic Bishops of
England and Wales, Ireland, and Scotland.*[6])

Confirmation is one of the seven sacraments of the
Church, but how did it develop? As we have seen, in the
early Church there was a single celebration of initiation,
with immersion in water followed almost immediately by
a rite of public 'sealing' by the bishop. Together, Baptism
and Confirmation formed what St Cyprian called a
'double sacrament'. Gradually, this second rite became
separated in time from Baptism. The bishop was less and
less able to be present at all Baptisms to seal and
complete them, especially when Christianity spread from
the towns into the countryside, adult Baptisms increased
once the Christian faith became accepted in the Empire,
infant Baptism became more general, and missionaries
baptised converts from paganism in areas far away from
any bishop. In the Eastern Church (and in much of France
and Spain), the problem was solved by allowing priests to

celebrate the whole rite of initiation, including Confirmation, although always using chrism consecrated by a bishop. The diocese of Rome continued to reserve Confirmation to its bishop, and this Roman practice was gradually established throughout most of the Western Church, partly through the influence of missionaries and scholars from the English Church which had adopted the Roman practice from the beginning.

Until the two sacraments became separated in time, little thought was given to the distinct meaning and contribution of Confirmation. The eventual separation led to some serious thinking about the way Confirmation 'sealed' and 'perfected' Baptism. This led gradually to the developed teaching which we now find in the Church's official documents.

We know, then, that Confirmation is intrinsically linked with Baptism, and that we cannot understand what Confirmation means apart from Baptism. We also know that Confirmation is a distinct sacrament of the Church, which contributes something of its own along the Christian path of initiation.

CONFIRMATION SEALS US WITH THE GIFT OF THE HOLY SPIRIT

In the Old Testament, the Spirit is the active, creative power of God. God spoke to his people through individual prophets, each inspired by his Spirit. But God promised the Day of the Lord when he would pour out his Spirit on everyone:

> Then afterward
> I will pour out my spirit on all flesh;
> your sons and your daughters shall prophesy,
> your old men shall dream dreams,
> and your young men shall see visions.
> Even on the male and female slaves,
> in those days, I will pour out my spirit. (*Joel* 2:28-29)

Christians understand the extraordinary events of the day of Pentecost as in some sense the fulfilment of Joel's prophecy (cf. *Acts* 2:14-21). This continues to happen today in a special way through the sacrament of Confirmation.

We come to be confirmed not just to receive the *gifts* of the Holy Spirit, but to be sealed with the *Gift* of the Holy Spirit. We receive the Holy Spirit in person. But is there a problem here? We have already received the Holy Spirit at our Baptism!

Confirmation is not simply a rite remembering and celebrating the fact that we received the Holy Spirit at our Baptism. Confirmation is a distinct sacrament, and involves in some way a special effect of God's presence in our lives. On the other hand, we must not talk about receiving the Holy Spirit at Confirmation in a way which underplays the giving of the Spirit at our Baptism. The creative power of God's Spirit is at work in us even before we are baptised, from the moment of our conception. We cannot even say 'Jesus is Lord' except under the influence of the Holy Spirit (*1 Corinthians* 12:3). The Holy Spirit is given in Baptism as the power of cleansing, regeneration and adoption, binding the believer into the 'fellowship of the Holy Spirit' which is the Church of Christ. The baptised person is someone immersed, plunged, soaked through, steeped in the Spirit. At our Baptism, the Holy Spirit was given to us fully.

The Holy Spirit is a Divine Person. We cannot have degrees of the Spirit, or receive more of him. But we can receive the Gift of the Spirit in different ways for different purposes, just as we can experience another human being in different ways for different reasons. There is no difficulty in the idea of the Spirit being 'given' several times to one person for distinct purposes. The Spirit works not only in various ways in different people (*1 Corinthians* 12:4-11), but also in various ways in the same person. Great Christian thinkers such as St

Irenaeus and St Augustine had no problem in affirming two 'givings' of the Holy Spirit in Christian initiation, one in the immersion in water and another in the rite of 'sealing', after the Baptism.

St Paul and St Luke provide the foundations for this idea of a double-giving of the Spirit. For St Paul, the Spirit is fully given at Baptism as the power of faith in believers enabling them to live the Christian life as people truly one 'in Christ'. For St Luke in the Acts of the Apostles, the Spirit is sometimes seen given in a special way after Baptism in the name of the Lord Jesus, suggesting that believers are somehow incomplete without this gift. We should be careful not to read too much into these texts, but St Luke's theology of the Holy Spirit in the Church is very important for understanding the precise meaning of Confirmation as a sealing of Baptism.

If you are preparing to be confirmed, what will this special giving of the Holy Spirit mean for you? It will not mean you receive 'more' of the Spirit, as if his presence were like a liquid ladled out in increasing quantities. The Spirit you have already received at your Baptism will 'seal' you, and work within you in a new way as you are drawn deeper into the life and work of the Church. You will be 'gifted' in a new way by receiving the Gift of the Spirit in person, and his presence within you will be powerfully fruitful in your life - if you say and live a true 'Yes' to that presence.

THE SEVEN GIFTS OF THE HOLY SPIRIT

wisdom   understanding   counsel

fortitude   knowledge   piety   fear of the Lord

(cf. *Isaiah* 11:2-3; *CCC,* no. 1831)

THE TWELVE FRUITS OF THE HOLY SPIRIT

charity   joy   peace   patience

kindness   goodness   generosity   gentleness

faithfulness   modesty   self-control   chastity

(cf. *Galatians* 5:22-23; *CCC,* no. 1832)

'God is love', and love is his first gift,
containing all others.
'God's love has been poured into our hearts
through the Holy Spirit who has been given to us.'

(*CCC,* no. 733, quoting *1 John* 4:8 and *Romans* 5:5)

You will be 'sealed' with a permanent marker. In the past, and sometimes even today, very important documents were sealed. Like Baptism, Confirmation is a once-in-a-lifetime experience. God does something deep in our lives which will never leave us. He places his own royal seal upon us, the Gift of the Holy Spirit. It is a sign that we belong to him, and that he has given his own self to us. This seal, sometimes called the 'sacramental character', is the sign 'that Jesus Christ has marked a Christian with the seal of his Spirit by clothing him with power from on high so that he may be his witness' (*CCC*, no. 1304).

At Confirmation, we are marked out permanently for Christ by the Gift of the Holy Spirit. But we should not take for granted the presence of the Spirit in our lives. Prayer for the coming of the Spirit should be central to our prayer each day. We ask God to renew the Spirit of holiness within us. If the Holy Spirit is really present in us, we will live holy lives, full of love for God and for one another.

Come Holy Spirit

The best way to prepare for Confirmation, or to renew the grace of Confirmation you have already received, is to pray for the Spirit to 'come' to you in a deeper way. The Holy Spirit is the Spirit of Holiness, the Spirit of Power, and above all the Spirit of Love. He is the deeply personal Spirit of Unity, who brings us closer to God and to each other. Perhaps use the following prayers, on your own or together with others. If you like singing, use a simple song asking for the Spirit to come to you, for example:

'Veni, Sancte Spiritus' (Come Holy Spirit) - there are well-known settings from the Taizé Community, and by Christopher Walker.

'Spirit of the living God, fall afresh on me'

Find a time and place where you can be quiet for a few moments. It may be in the church. It may be at home, or a few quiet moments at work or at school. Or go and sit in the park, or by the sea, or under a tree. Anywhere will do.

Firstly, quieten down for a moment. Relax your body and mind. Then focus on our Lord. Perhaps light a candle. Or look at a cross or icon. Spend a few moments in simple adoration and praise of God. Thank him for being there with you. Lift up your heart to him. Tell him you worship and adore him.

Then ask the Holy Spirit to come to you. Quietly, with pauses of silent waiting, invite the Spirit into your mind - into your thoughts and memories. Invite him into your body, from head to toe. Invite him deep into your heart and soul. Ask the Spirit to fill your whole being with God's own love and peace. Sit there quietly, knowing that God always gives his Holy Spirit when we ask him.

Then invite the Spirit into each member of your family in turn. Ask God to fill with his love your husband or wife, your parents and children, your brothers and sisters, your friends and neighbours. Pray for each of them by name. Invite him into each of your special relationships (with your girlfriend or boyfriend, and your other close friends). Ask him to bless your love with his.

Finally, invite the Spirit to fill your home with his presence. Ask him to come into your home as he did at Pentecost.

Then finish by praising God once more. Perhaps simply say:

'Glory be to the Father, and to the Son, and to the Holy Spirit, as it was in the beginning, is now, and ever shall be, world without end. Amen.'

CONFIRMATION UNITES US MORE CLOSELY
TO THE CHURCH

Sometimes Confirmation has been seen as little more than a special ceremony when we renew our commitment to Jesus, perhaps for the first time standing on our own two feet, and when God gives us an 'increase of grace' to help us live out our faith in a world which doesn't exactly make it easy to be a real Christian. This great sacrament is an opportunity for both of these things, but it is much more than that!

Confirmation seals and perfects what happened to us at our Baptism. When we were baptised, we were welcomed into the community of Christ's Church, into the family of the friends and followers of Jesus. Confirmation draws us deeper into the worship, life and work of the Church. Far from being the time when we begin to opt out of the Church and its worship (especially Sunday Mass), Confirmation is the moment when Christ binds us more closely to his Church.

There is no point being confirmed
unless we want to be more fully 'churched'!

There are degrees of membership, of belonging to the Church. It all begins at Baptism. When we first receive Holy Communion, we are drawn more deeply into the Church's life. And all the official teaching documents tells us that by Confirmation we are 'bound more perfectly to the Church.' The Holy Spirit is the Spirit of Unity, the Spirit of Communion. At Confirmation, the Spirit 'seals', strengthens, confirms and perfects our unity with Christ's Church, and draws us more deeply into the fullness of its mystery.

> By the sacrament of Confirmation,
> they are more perfectly bound to the Church
> and are endowed with the special strength of the
> Holy Spirit. (*Second Vatican Council.*[7])

If you are preparing to be confirmed, ask yourself a vital question. Do you really want to be more fully a member of the Church, more involved in the life and work of the Church? Are you ready to be more truly 'churched' by the Holy Spirit? You may have no idea at the moment in what special ways you will one day serve Christ in the world, but you are certainly someone called to serve. At this very moment, the Risen Jesus is calling you by name, calling you to himself, calling you so that he can send you out into the world in his name. This involves being called into the community of his friends and followers. The call to follow Jesus is always a call to belong to the family of God, to be a living member of the Body of Christ, a living stone in the Temple of the Holy Spirit. Being 'churched' lies at the heart of being a true Christian, and being more fully 'churched' lies at the heart of the meaning of Confirmation. Confirmation will make you as full a member of the Church as your parents or your parish priest or your bishop!

Whether or not you have already been confirmed, think about the meaning and purpose of the Church. Any Confirmation preparation will involve a serious look at what the Church is and what it is called to be and do for the Lord. How you understand the Church affects how you understand yourself. The Church is not primarily a building, or an institution. Together, we are the Church, and by your Baptism you are a vital and essential member of the Church. Without you, the Church cannot be fully itself. Without the Church, you cannot be fully yourself.

'You are a chosen race, a royal priesthood,
a holy nation, God's own people,
in order that you may proclaim the mighty acts of him
who has called you out of darkness
into his marvellous light.' (*1 Peter* 2:9)

'Let no-one diminish the church gathering
by his or her absence, that the Body of Christ
may not be diminished by one member.
Do not tear apart the Body of Christ.'[8]

CONFIRMATION COMMISSIONS US
FOR PUBLIC WITNESS

By Confirmation, a baptised person is taken more fully into the mystery of the Church. But what does that really mean? Into what aspect of the mystery of the Church is a person initiated by Confirmation, if not as something totally new then at least in a radically intensified and empowered way? What lies at the very heart of the mystery, meaning and mission of the Church, something into which we can be further initiated and drawn more deeply by being confirmed? What is the Church really for?

Pope Paul VI gave us the heart of the answer in his letter on proclaiming the Gospel (*Evangelii Nuntiandi*) in 1975: 'Evangelising is in fact the grace and vocation proper to the Church, her deepest identity' (no. 14). Evangelising means proclaiming the Gospel, the Good News of Jesus Christ, by what we say, by what we do, and by the way we live.

> 'Evangelisation is in fact the grace and vocation proper to the Church, her deepest identity.' (*Pope Paul VI.*[9])

Every Christian is called to bear witness to Jesus Christ, even before being confirmed. In some special way, however, the Sacrament of Confirmation consecrates and strengthens us to share in the public mission of the Church. We can understand this most clearly by going back to Jesus himself and his very first followers.

Scripture Reflections

One way to focus on the meaning of Confirmation is to reflect on three key passages from the Gospels. Whether you are working in a group or on your own, begin by spending a few moments in quiet prayer. Focus on the Lord Jesus. Ask him to pour out his Spirit upon you. Ask the Holy Spirit to be in your mind and heart and soul as you read each passage. Ask God to speak to you through these words which are the word of God himself. Then read the passage slowly and prayerfully. If it helps, imagine yourself being there in the story. Take the part of one of the people waiting to be baptised in the River Jordan by John the Baptist, or one of the apostles in the Upper Room. Then spend a few moments in silence again. What is God saying to you in this passage? Write down any thoughts you have. If you are in a group, share them with each other. Once you have done all this, then read the short reflection given after the passage. Finish by a time of prayer. Ask Jesus to give you the inner strength to live what you hear him call you to be and to do.

The Baptism of Jesus (Mark 1:9-20)

'In those days Jesus came from Nazareth of Galilee and was baptised by John in the Jordan. And just as he was coming up out of the water, he saw the heavens torn apart and the Spirit descending like a dove on him. And a voice came from heaven, "You are my Son, the Beloved; with you I am well pleased."

'And the Spirit immediately drove him out into the wilderness. He was in the wilderness forty days, tempted by Satan; and he was with the wild beasts; and the angels waited on him. Now after John was arrested, Jesus came to Galilee, proclaiming the good news of God, and saying, "The time is fulfilled, and the kingdom of God has come near; repent, and believe in the good news."

'As Jesus passed along the Sea of Galilee, he saw Simon and his brother Andrew casting a net into the sea - for they were fishermen. And Jesus said to them, "Follow me and I will make you fish for people." And immediately they left their nets and followed him. As he went a little farther, he saw James son of Zebedee and his brother John, who were in their boat mending the nets. Immediately he called them; and they left their father Zebedee in the boat with the hired men, and followed him.'

Reflection

Jesus was already the Son of God, full of the Holy Spirit. His 'Baptism' was rather like our being 'confirmed'. God the Father re-affirmed Jesus as his beloved Son, and poured out his Spirit upon him. From that moment, after many years of living a quiet and hidden life, Jesus began his public ministry as the Servant of God.

By your Baptism, you are already the beloved daughter or son of God, filled with God's Holy Spirit. At your Confirmation, God anoints you in a special way with his Spirit. It is a chance to re-commit yourself to God as a member of his family and a follower of Jesus, renewing your Baptismal promises. But it is also the moment when your own 'public ministry' begins, slowly but surely. Jesus himself calls you personally, by name, to work side by side with him, to share his mission, to be his friend and disciple.

The Resurrection (John 20:19-29)

'When it was evening on that day, the first day of the week, and the doors of the house where the disciples had met were locked for fear of the Jews, Jesus came and stood among them and said, "Peace be with you." After he said this, he showed them his hands and his side. Then the disciples rejoiced when they saw the Lord. Jesus said to them again, "Peace be with you. As the Father has sent me, so I send you." When he had said this, he breathed on them and said to them, "Receive the Holy Spirit. If you forgive the sins of any, they are forgiven them; if you retain the sins of any, they are retained." But Thomas (who was called the Twin), one of the twelve, was not with them when Jesus came. So the other disciples told him, "We have seen the Lord." But he said to them, "Unless I see the mark of the nails in his hands, and put my finger in the mark of the nails and my hand in his side, I will not believe." A week later his disciples were again in the house, and Thomas was with them. Although the doors were shut, Jesus came and stood among them and said, "Peace be with you." Then he said to Thomas, "Put your finger here and see my hands. Reach out your hand and put it in my side. Do not doubt but believe." Thomas answered him, "My Lord and my God!" Jesus said to him, "Have you believed because you have seen me? Blessed are those who have not seen and yet have come to believe.'"

Reflection

The apostles know Jesus has been crucified, and they are naturally scared of going outside. They might be arrested and crucified too! So they lock themselves in and hide away. They are probably also feeling guilty that they abandoned Jesus at the crunch moment, even denying they knew him. But Jesus still comes to them. His first words are not of condemnation, but of peace: "Shalom" he says, "Peace be with you". Despite their previous lack of courage, he says to them, "As the Father has sent me, so I send you." Then he breathes on them and says, "Receive the Holy Spirit."

We may be much like the apostles. Part of us wants to know Jesus, to be close to him and committed to him, but another side of us is scared. We are afraid of what others may think of us, afraid of being laughed at, afraid of what it might all involve. It is not 'cool' to stand up as a Christian in today's world. Perhaps we have not been all that faithful to him until now. But Jesus' words to you are the same: "Peace - forget the past", and then he says to you those extraordinary words, "As the Father has sent me, so I send you." He wants you to work with him, bringing his presence to others. That demands tremendous inner strength and courage. It is easy to be like everyone else: to be a young man or young woman of God requires something extra, and Jesus will give you what you need if you let him. At your Confirmation he will anoint you and breathe on you, and say, "Receive the Holy Spirit." Pray daily for the coming of the Spirit into your life.

Most people are a bit like 'Doubting Thomas'. We need to see before we believe. But where can we see the 'hands and side of Jesus' today? That is our role - to show Jesus to others by our lives. You may have doubts yourself - you probably do. But don't forget, no matter how closed and locked our doors may be at times, Jesus himself is always there with us.

Pentecost (Acts 2:1-13)

'When the day of Pentecost had come, they were all together in one place. And suddenly from heaven there came a sound like the rush of a violent wind, and it filled the entire house where they were sitting. Divided tongues, as of fire, appeared among them, and a tongue rested on each of them. All of them were filled with the Holy Spirit and began to speak in other languages, as the Spirit gave them ability. Now there were devout Jews from every nation under heaven living in Jerusalem. And at this sound the crowd gathered and was bewildered, because each one heard them speaking in the native language of each. Amazed and astonished, they asked, "Are not all these who are speaking Galileans? And how is it that we hear, each of us, in our own native language? Parthians, Medes, Elamites, and residents of Mesopotamia, Judea and Cappadocia, Pontus and Asia, Phrygia and Pamphylia, Egypt and the parts of Libya belonging to Cyrene, and visitors from Rome, both Jews and proselytes, Cretans and Arabs - in our own languages we hear them speaking about God's deeds of power." All were amazed and perplexed, saying to one another, "What does this mean?" But others sneered and said, "They are filled with new wine."'

Reflection

Yet again, the apostles were all huddled together in the Upper Room, afraid to go out. It is almost as though God came along and shook them out of their house, and fired them up to go outside to bear witness to their faith in Jesus. It is much easier to stay indoors, to keep one's faith private. But if you let the Spirit come upon you, he will lead you from your own 'upper room' into the outside world, to bear public witness to your faith in Jesus. Your friends and family might well be 'amazed and perplexed' too, and perhaps even think you are drunk or mad! God will give you the best possible 'gift of tongues', the grace to proclaim the Risen Jesus to everyone by your words, your deeds, and the way you live.

'the sacrament of Confirmation... in a certain way perpetuates the grace of Pentecost in the Church.'
(*Pope Paul VI.*[10])

Go public

A clear theme ties together these three passages: the Holy Spirit is given to us so that we can 'go public' with our faith. Bearing public witness to our faith, proclaiming it in the market square or the shopping centre, from the housetops and in our lives, is essential to being a person who is a full follower of Jesus, a full member of the Church.

The Church has been called 'the universal sacrament of salvation'. This is a very pithy definition of what the Church is for - to be for people everywhere a powerful sign and instrument of all that Jesus came to achieve by his life, death and resurrection. The Church is a community both of worship and witness. It is not a gathering of individual and private believers, but a visible community called to public worship and public witness. We are not fully 'churched' unless we are involved in both.

> It is the whole Church that receives the mission to evangelise, and the work of each individual member is important for the whole. (*Pope Paul VI.*[11])

It is into this all-embracing missionary nature of the Church that a person is visibly drawn by being confirmed. All the teaching documents of the Catholic Church, and the rite of Confirmation itself, show how central the ideas of evangelisation and witness are to our 'official' understanding of this great sacrament.

Back to the Bible

This teaching on Confirmation is rooted in St Luke's presentation of the role of the Holy Spirit in the Church. For St Luke, the present age is one of missionary activity by a prophetic community empowered by the Holy Spirit. Jesus said to his apostles: 'you will receive power when the Holy Spirit has come upon you, and you will be my witnesses... to the ends of the earth' (*Acts* 1:8). This promise was fulfilled at Pentecost, and continues to be fulfilled today especially through the sacrament of Confirmation. In a way, Confirmation is for us today what Pentecost was for the apostles. The most notable effect of Pentecost was not the 'wonders' associated with it, but the way in which frightened disciples were transformed into courageous witnesses to the Risen Lord.

They were filled with power from on high, the enabling, strengthening and inspiring power of God's love which we call the Holy Spirit.

Pentecost reveals what must always lie at the very heart of the mystery of the Church. Evangelisation, proclaiming the Gospel, is of its very essence, but this is possible only by the power of the Spirit. The Holy Spirit is the Evangeliser, the Witness who testifies on behalf of Christ (*John* 15:26). Jesus promised the Spirit from the Father, and said to his Apostles: 'You also are to testify because you have been with me from the beginning' (*John* 15:27). By anointing us with the Gift of the Spirit at Confirmation, he calls each of us to testify. Through Confirmation, the Holy Spirit draws us into the Church's deepest identity and mystery, and shares with us his own witness to Christ before the world.

Our Baptism gave us a responsibility for bearing witness to our faith. Confirmation takes that responsibility a stage further, into the public realm. Like the apostles from their Upper Room, the confirmed Christian is called to come out into the open in an active and positive way, not only to defend and preserve their faith but as someone publicly and 'officially' sent forth by Christ in his Church. The apostles themselves were already witnesses to Christ before Pentecost, but the Gift of the Spirit empowered them for full witness before the nations. I have suggested a parallel with Christ's Baptism in the Jordan: he was already the Spirit-filled servant Son of the Father, but his anointing with the Spirit in the Jordan launched his three-year public ministry as the Messiah and Saviour.

Ambassadors for Christ

St Paul gets to the heart of the matter by calling us 'ambassadors for Christ':

'So if anyone is in Christ, there is a new creation: everything old has passed away; see, everything has become new! All this is from God, who reconciled us to himself through Christ, and has given us the ministry of reconciliation; that is, in Christ God was reconciling the world to himself, not counting their trespasses against them, and entrusting the message of reconciliation to us. So we are ambassadors for Christ, since God is making his appeal through us; we entreat you on behalf of Christ, be reconciled to God.' (*2 Corinthians* 5:17-20).

Every citizen of a country is expected to be a private ambassador, but being made an official ambassador gives one's witness a power and authority which is radically new. At Confirmation, we become ambassadors for Christ - his public representatives, envoys, spokespeople. The Risen Jesus wishes to appeal to others through us, speak through us, work through us. He seeks to make all things new. Prepare for your Confirmation, or renew your Confirmation commitment, by allowing Christ to make you a new creation, and then be his instrument in renewing the earth.

Defend and spread the faith

Many Catholics were brought up with the idea that Confirmation makes us 'soldiers of Christ'. An influential sermon by Faustus of Riez (c.AD 460) saw Confirmation as arming baptised soldiers and giving them strength for the battle ahead. In the teaching of the Church through the centuries, however, witnessing to Christ is far more central than being a soldier. In times of persecution, it is only natural that a rather defensive understanding prevails. We need strength to hold onto our faith against all those who seek to undermine it - whether non-Christians, other Christians or all the worldly influences around us today. But we are called to do much more than simply hold onto our faith and keep it intact. As a Christian poster once put it, 'Don't just keep the faith - spread it!' The New Testament calls us to a positive and joyful proclamation of the Risen Lord to all the world. It is essential that we keep intact our Catholic faith. We need strength and courage to endure and persevere, especially in today's world when even our friends may laugh at us or mock us for trying to live as Christians.

The temptation is to stay safe in our 'Upper Room', and avoid the risk of being attacked by those outside. But the Holy Spirit will have none of that! Jesus sends us forth to proclaim the Good News, to bear witness to him, to draw others to him. In times of persecution, it is all too easy to lose a sense of mission, and to concentrate on 'defence' rather than 'witness'. The early Christians teach us that we can do both, if God's Spirit is with us.

Some more history

This positive understanding of Confirmation has been central to Catholic teaching throughout the centuries. Around AD 800, Alcuin of York, the English adviser to the great Emperor Charlemagne, wrote that Confirmation candidates 'receive the Spirit of seven-fold grace so that they may be strengthened by the Holy Spirit to preach to others.' This idea of the gift of boldness in confessing Christ passed into the thinking of all the great medieval writers. St Thomas Aquinas recognised that a spiritual power different to that of Baptism was given at Confirmation: 'Just as the baptised receive spiritual power to confess their faith by the reception of other sacraments, so also those who are confirmed receive the power publicly, and as it were officially, to profess faith in Christ in their speech.' St Thomas drew out this official, public character of the witness for which the confirmed person is commissioned: 'the sacrament is given that we may freely confess our faith, but not in an elementary way as is the case in Baptism.'

This understanding was affirmed by the Council of Florence in 1439 in its summary of what remains today official Catholic teaching: 'The effect of this sacrament is that the Holy Spirit is given in it for strengthening as he was given to the apostles on the day of Pentecost, so that Christians may boldly confess the name of Christ.' The anointing is given to Christians 'lest they be embarrassed to confess the name of Christ and especially his cross...'

Enriched by a renewed stress on the intimate link between Baptism and Confirmation, and by a deeper understanding of the 'churchly' character of the sacraments, this 'witness' understanding of Confirmation passed into the teaching of the Second Vatican Council and the revised rite of Confirmation. The suggested homily and intercessions, one of the opening prayers and the prayer over the people for the Mass of Confirmation, all include reference to being sent forth to witness. The 1971 Apostolic Constitution promulgating the new rite simply quotes Vatican II to the effect that by confirmation the baptised 'are bound more closely to the Church and are more strictly obliged to spread and defend the faith by word and deed as true witnesses to Christ.'

You Must be Witnesses before All the World

This is the homily given in the text of the Rite of Confirmation. (The bishop may use these or similar words.)

On the day of Pentecost, the apostles received the Holy Spirit as the Lord had promised. They also received the power of giving the Holy Spirit to others and so completing the work of Baptism. This we read in the Acts of the Apostles. When Saint Paul placed his hands on those who had been baptised, the Holy Spirit came upon them, and they began to speak in other languages and in prophetic words.

Bishops are successors of the apostles, and have this power of giving the Holy Spirit to the baptised, either personally or through the priests they appoint.

In our day, the coming of the Holy Spirit in Confirmation is no longer marked by the gift of tongues, but we know his coming by faith. He fills our hearts with the love of God, brings us together in one faith but in different vocations, and works within us to make the Church one and holy.

The Gift of the Holy Spirit which you are to receive will be a spiritual sign and seal to make you more like Christ and more perfect members of the Church. At his

Baptism by John, Christ himself was anointed by the Spirit and sent out on his public ministry to set the world on fire.

You have already been baptised into Christ, and now you will receive the power of his Spirit and the sign of the cross on your forehead. You must be witnesses before all the world to his suffering, death, and resurrection. Your way of life should at all times reflect the goodness of Christ. Christ gives varied gifts to his Church, and the Spirit distributes them among the members of Christ's body to build up the holy people of God in unity and love.

Be active members of the Church, alive in Jesus Christ. Under the guidance of the Holy Spirit, give your lives completely in the service of all, as did Christ, who came not to be served but to serve.

This interpretation of Confirmation as a sacramental commissioning for public witness to Christ in no way undermines its initiatory character or its essential link with Baptism. Our initiation into the mystery of Christ in the Church is sealed and completed precisely by our being anointed with the Holy Spirit and commissioned for official public witness.

Though a distinct sacramental rite, a true and proper sacrament of the Church, Confirmation is an integral part of the process of Christian initiation, closely linked to Baptism which it seals and perfects. A special giving of the Holy Spirit seals our Baptism precisely by uniting baptised people more closely to the Church as a visible sacrament of Christ; it commissions them for full responsibility in the public witness and evangelisation which constitutes the Church's deepest identity, and it gives the strength and power needed for this new status in the community. Far from being contradictory, the initiatory and witness aspects of Confirmation are complementary.

Perhaps one reason why Confirmation has been undervalued is the impoverished awareness which many Christians have of the full mystery of the Church, and of the centrality of evangelisation to its whole identity and purpose. The sacrament of Confirmation, as the sealing of Baptismal initiation, affirms visibly that mission and witness are of the essence of Christian discipleship.

What does Confirmation Do for Us?

Some teaching from the *Catechism of the Catholic Church*.

'By Confirmation Christians, that is, those who are anointed, share more completely in the mission of Jesus Christ and the fullness of the Holy Spirit with which he is filled, so that their lives may give off "the aroma of Christ".' (no. 1294)

'Confirmation brings an increase and deepening of Baptismal grace:
- it roots us more deeply in the divine filiation which makes us cry, "Abba! Father!";
- it unites us more firmly to Christ;
- it increases the gifts of the Holy Spirit in us;
- it renders our bond with the Church more perfect;
- it gives us a special strength of the Holy Spirit to spread and defend the faith by word and action as true witnesses of Christ, to confess the name of Christ boldly, and never be ashamed of the Cross.' (no. 1303)

'Its effect is to unite those who receive it more closely to the Church, to her apostolic origins, and to her mission of bearing witness to Christ.' (no. 1313)

'Confirmation perfects Baptismal grace; it is the sacrament which gives the Holy Spirit in order to root us more deeply in the divine filiation, incorporate us more firmly into Christ, strengthen our bond with the Church, associate us more closely with her mission, and help us bear witness to the Christian faith in words accompanied by deeds.' (no. 1316)

Sharing God's Mission

Confirmation draws us more deeply into the Holy Spirit's mission in the world, the mission to witness to Christ as the one sent by the Father. We are welcomed more fully into a Spirit-filled community called to share God's own mission to his people.

Above all, the sacrament of Confirmation is rooted in the life of God. What kind of God do we believe in as Christians? The ultimate Christian answer is the Holy Trinity. Some religions see God as a rather isolated figure who lives enclosed in his own heavenly 'Upper Room', occasionally speaking or reaching down to us when really necessary. Christians believe that God has revealed himself to be very different. The very nature of God is self-giving Love. We believe in a God who is eternally giving himself, pouring himself out and 'sending' himself. God is an outreaching God, a 'missionary' God.

Unless we are deeply aware of God's 'missionary', outreaching, self-giving love, we can so easily justify parishes which are wonderful worshipping communities, but which are not truly aflame with a Pentecostal passion for proclaiming the Good News of the Risen Jesus outside of their cosy 'upper rooms'.

What on earth is the Church really for? What is the mission of the Church? Strictly speaking, the Church has no mission of its own. The Church is a community taken up by God the Father as a sign and instrument of his sending of the Son and the Holy Spirit. The whole Church, and each parish community, is called to share in the mission of Christ and the mission of the Holy Spirit, the mission of God himself.

If we are really united with Jesus Christ, we cannot but be missionary! Jesus Christ is in person God's missionary outreach to us, his Eternal Word. When we become one body and one blood with Jesus in receiving Holy Communion, we become more united with Christ as the One being sent by the Father to save the world. We become drawn more deeply into his mission. We cannot chose to be united with Jesus but not to share his work! There is no room for a vision of the Church as simply a community of believers who pray and worship together, and love one another, but who have no desire to be drawn into the continuing work of the Risen Lord to bring his saving love to every human being in every time and place. True Catholic life is of course centred on the Mass, but Mass and Mission belong together. The celebration of Mass may end after the priest's blessing, but our mission continues, above all because our communion with Christ himself and his saving work has been renewed and enlivened. We are sent in peace 'to love and to serve the Lord.'

At the end of Mass, we are sent forth in peace to love and to serve the Lord, in deeper communion, we hope, with each other and with the whole Church. We receive the body of Christ so that we may go forth as the Body of Christ into the world, the living sacrament of his presence in the midst of others. Through the Eucharist we become more profoundly the Church and we are sent forth as the Church to fulfil our mission in and for the world. Here is an intimate and inseparable unity between Mass and mission, between worship and way of life. Our communion with Christ means that we share not only his life but also his mission. At each Eucharist, the Risen Christ says to us anew: 'As the Father sent me, so am I sending you', and breathes his Spirit upon us. The Spirit we receive anoints us afresh to bring good news to the poor, since any true communion with the living Lord will lead us to recognise him in those most in need. (*Catholic Bishops of England and Wales, Ireland, and Scotland.*[12])

Our understanding of God and his Church should be rooted in St John's great summary of the Good News: 'God so loved the world that he gave his only Son' (*John 3:16*). This is God's mission statement, and the Church's too! Confirmation draws us more deeply into the mystery of God's giving of his Son to the world.

Disciple and Witness to Christ

Following Christ involves being prepared to witness to him. A true disciple is someone who both stays close to the Lord and is sent out into the world by him. Jesus says to each of us: "Come to me" and "Go in my name". But how can we bear witness to Christ? This will depend on our age, our state of life, our particular gifts and talents. But we are all called, each in our own way, to be living signs and instruments of our Lord to others, and to proclaim the Good News, the Gospel, to them. We do this in many different ways.

By what I say

Firstly, we bear witness to Christ by what we say. We should be open about our faith in him, and 'go public' with that faith. That can be difficult in our society, which can seem to have little time for spiritual things. But there are times when we should talk openly about what we believe, and share our faith in Jesus with others. Catholics need to be much more ready to profess their faith openly, publicly. We are called to be heralds of Christ, announcing the Good News of his saving love. We are called to be prophets: God has chosen to speak through us. We can be his voice in the world, and speak his word to people. One of the Eucharistic Prefaces at Mass puts it well: the Church was founded to be the sign on earth of God's infinite holiness, and as the living Gospel for all to hear.[13] As Pope John XXIII once said, 'You are the only Bible that someone may ever read'.

By what I do

Secondly, we bear witness to Christ by what we do, above all by our acts of loving kindness to those in any kind of need. Like Christ himself, we are called 'not to be served but to serve'. Jesus calls us to follow his own example of humble love in washing the feet of his disciples. Some Confirmation preparation programmes involve an element of service to others - perhaps visiting and helping the sick or elderly. After Confirmation, we should seek active ways to show our love. The Parable of the Good Samaritan challenges us to stop and care for those in need, rather than pass by on the other side: "Go and do likewise", Jesus says to us (*Luke* 10:25-37). Jesus teaches us that whatever we do for the least of his brothers and sisters, we do for him, and gives the examples of feeding the hungry, welcoming the stranger, clothing the naked, caring for the sick and visiting those in prison (*Matthew* 25:31-46). We need to find our own way of loving and serving Christ in the poor and the needy.

We live in God's world. He shares with us his dominion over creation, but we are only his caretakers, his stewards. We have a responsibility to take care of our planet, to make it a better world, not just for ourselves but for all people and for the generations to come. The world, its atmosphere and its resources are not ours to do with as we please. In everything we do, we are called to put into practice our prayer to the Creator that his will be done on earth. Being confirmed commits us more strongly to care for the environment, to careful stewarding of God's world and all its people.

And we are called to work for justice. The Spirit we receive at Confirmation is the same Spirit who anointed Jesus for his mission as the Messiah. Jesus applies to himself the words of Isaiah:

> The Spirit of the Lord is upon me,
> because he has anointed me
> to bring good news to the poor.
> He has sent me to proclaim release to captives,
> and recovery of sight to the blind,
> to let the oppressed go free,
> to proclaim the year of the Lord's favour.
> (*Luke* 4:16f; cf. *Isaiah* 61:1f)

Because we are united with Christ, we receive the same Spirit, and the same words are said to us.

God challenges us through the Old Testament prophets to be just and to work for justice. Jesus takes this teaching for granted, and demands an active love for those in need. We find the same teaching throughout two thousand years of the Church, often put in a very challenging and disturbing way. The social teaching of the Popes of the last hundred years makes it very clear that working for justice and peace is no optional extra; it lies at the very heart of our mission to proclaim the Good News of God's liberating love. The call to public witness includes a summons to speak out for justice, to do all we can to defend and promote human rights, to work for freedom and peace for every human being. Pope John Paul II called those about to be confirmed to be 'devoted to the work of justice, which will bring peace on earth'. There are many practical ways in our society to work for justice, in our own country and overseas. See what you can do for the homeless and for refugees and asylum seekers. Work for justice for the disabled in our society. Do all you can to protect the weak and vulnerable, especially unborn children, and the sick and elderly. Speak out against any kind of bullying or discrimination. Denounce the evil of racism wherever it occurs. Share your own resources, your money, your time, your talents, with those in need. Get involved with CAFOD in its work for overseas development. Work with Amnesty International for prisoners of conscience and people being tortured. Join your local Justice and Peace Group, or try to form one in your school or college or parish. Above all, act justly in all your dealings with others.

At the Confirmation Mass, candidates are asked to stand up in front of everyone else. Being confirmed commits us to stand up for what is right and just, no matter what the consequences may be. Archbishop Oscar Romero is an example and inspiration for many people. In 1980, he was murdered while saying Mass in El Salvador because he refused to be silent about the abuse of human rights in his country. Jesus promised the help of the Holy Spirit in the face of opposition and persecution (*Luke* 12:11-12). The Greek word for 'witness' is *martyr*! We will probably not be called to martyrdom in the usual sense, but all of us need to be ready to stand up for Christ 'for better for worse'. We can only do that if we have the strength of the Holy Spirit within us.

Pope John Paul II to Confirmation candidates at Coventry, 1982

'Christ's gift of the Holy Spirit is going to be poured out upon you in a particular way. You will hear the words of the Church spoken over you, calling upon the Holy Spirit to confirm your faith, to seal you in love, to strengthen you for his service. You will then take your place among fellow-citizens throughout the world, full citizens now of the People of God. You will witness to the truth of the Gospel in the name of Jesus Christ. You will live your lives in such a way as to make holy all human life. Together with all the confirmed, you will become living stones in the cathedral of peace. Indeed, you are called by God to be instruments of his peace.

'Today you must understand that you are not alone. We are one body, one people, one Church of Christ. The sponsor who stands by your side represents for you the whole community. Together, with a great crowd of witnesses drawn from all peoples and every age, you represent Christ.

'You are young people who have received a mission from Christ, for he says to you today: 'As the Father sent me, so I am sending you.'

'On that first Pentecost, our Saviour gave the Apostles the power to forgive sins when he poured into their hearts the gift of the Holy Spirit. The same Holy Spirit comes to you today in the Sacrament of Confirmation, to involve you more completely in the Church's fight against sin and in her mission of fostering holiness. He comes to dwell more fully in your hearts and to strengthen you for the struggle with evil.

'My dear young people, the world of today needs you, for it needs men and women who are filled with the Holy Spirit. It needs your courage and hopefulness, your faith and perseverance. The world of tomorrow will be built by you. Today you receive the gift of the Holy Spirit so that you may work with deep faith and with abiding love, so that you may help to bring to the world the fruits of reconciliation and peace. Strengthened by the Holy Spirit and his manifold gifts, commit yourselves wholeheartedly to the Church's struggle against sin.

'Strive to be unselfish: try not to be obsessed with material things. Be active members of the People of God. Be reconciled with each other, and devoted to the work of justice, which will bring peace on earth.

'On the first day of Pentecost, the Holy Spirit came upon the Apostles and upon Mary and filled them with his power. Today we remember that moment, and we open ourselves again to the gift of that same Spirit. In that Spirit we are baptised. In that Spirit we are confirmed. In that Spirit we are called to share in the mission of Christ. In that Spirit we shall indeed become the People of Pentecost, the apostles of our time.'

Called to serve

We are anointed at Confirmation as a sign that God has set us aside for some special service of him in the world. Each of us is called to serve. Every one of us has a special part to play in God's plan for the world. St Paul teaches us that every member of the Church is vital and essential, and each of us has received gifts of service from the Spirit

(*1 Corinthians* 12:1-31). Our Baptism and Confirmation mean that we are very precious to God. There can be no greater calling, no greater dignity, than to be God's own daughters and sons, members of God's royal family.

We each need to find what special call we have. Most of us will live out our Confirmation through the sacrament of Marriage, and the call to parenthood. It is precisely because Marriage is such a sacred way of living our Confirmation commitment that we should be confirmed before receiving the sacrament of Marriage. Some will be religious brothers and sisters. Others will be deacons, priests or bishops in the service of Christ's Church. Some will find their special vocation as single lay people. When deciding what we are going to do with our lives, we need to listen carefully to what God is saying to us - in the silent stirrings of our hearts, and through the wisdom and guidance of those around us.

By the way I live

We witness to Christ not only by our words and deeds, but above all by the kind of people we are and by the way of life we lead. Christ is the centre of our lives. Our values and priorities will be different to those of many people around us. We will be people who seek to give rather than to receive, to serve rather than to be served. The needs of people will be more important to us than a desire to have more for ourselves. Jesus calls us to live simply, and to share what we have. There is no room for unnecessary luxuries when so many of our fellow human beings do not even have enough to survive. We will be people known for our generosity of spirit, our willingness to share, our loving kindness, our passion for justice and right, our peace of heart, the strength of our gentleness, our refusal to give way to evil of any kind. We will be people who live by the spirit of the 'Beatitudes' given by Jesus in his Sermon on the Mount (*Matthew* 5), the spirit of joy, simplicity and mercy. Above all, we will be known for our love, and for our Gospel joy.

> Father...
> You renew your Church in every age
> by raising up men and women outstanding in holiness,
> living witnesses of your unchanging love.
> They inspire us by their heroic lives,
> and help us by their constant prayers
> to be the living sign of your saving power.[14]

Prayer and love

We can only live out our Confirmation if we stay in close touch with God. On our own, we know we are weak and we fall so easily. But for God, all things are possible. With the power of his presence within us, we can do great things for God. This is why our prayer is so vital. Daily prayer is essential if we are going to witness to Christ each and every day. Like the Apostles, we must spend time with our Lord if we are to be sent out by him. Find somewhere to pray each day. Perhaps call into your church on the way home from school or work. Spend time in prayerful adoration before Christ in the Blessed Sacrament. Or find a peaceful place somewhere else. Set aside a prayer corner in your house or bedroom. Whatever else you do in your prayer, ask God each day to anoint you afresh with his Holy Spirit. Ask him to fill your heart and soul, your mind and body, with his love and his life. Ask him to be close to you. Then your inner self will grow strong, and you will be rooted and planted in love. You will be able to bring the power of God's love to others, and help to change their lives, and to renew the earth. You will be God's voice to them, God's touch for them. Prayer and love belong together, and they are together the heart of the Christian life. Nothing will attract other people to you more than a love which comes from a pure heart, a heart which is God's own gift to you in prayer.

So when should we be Confirmed?

There are many different and conflicting views on the right age and stage for Confirmation. That discussion can take place elsewhere, although any decisions should be based first and foremost on a proper understanding of Catholic teaching on the sacrament. The *Catechism of the Catholic Church* highlights a few key points for deciding who is ready to be confirmed. Every baptised person should receive the sacrament of Confirmation 'at the appropriate time', because without Confirmation and the Eucharist, our Christian initiation remains incomplete (no. 1306).

What, then, is the appropriate time? 'A candidate for Confirmation, who has attained the age of reason, must profess the faith, be in the state of grace, have the intention of receiving the sacrament, and *be prepared to assume the role of disciple and witness to Christ, both within the ecclesial community and in temporal affairs*' (no. 1319; my italics). The last point is especially important, summing up the meaning of the sacrament and also the degree of spiritual maturity normally required in a candidate for 'the appropriate time' to have arrived. An earlier passage in the Catechism reminds us that preparation for Confirmation 'should aim at leading the Christian toward a more intimate union with Christ and a more lively familiarity with the Holy Spirit - his actions, his gifts, and his biddings - *in order to be more capable of assuming the apostolic responsibilities of Christian life*' (no.1309; my italics).

A smelly oil

Chrism is a deliberately smelly oil, a mixture of oil and perfume. People usually put on perfume when they are going out, not when they are staying in! The fragrance is designed to attract people to us. In recent years, they have been TV adverts for various 'smells' which seem to have a remarkable effect. A young woman walks down the street, and finds herself surrounded by men bearing flowers. Something similar should happen once we have been anointed with chrism at Confirmation. Our lives should be fragrant with the Spirit of holiness, and give off the 'aroma of Christ'. Other people should be attracted to Christ through our words and deeds, and through the powerful silent witness of the way we live our lives.

One form of the blessing of chrism at the Chrism Mass sums up much of the challenge of being confirmed:

By anointing them with the Spirit,
you strengthen all who have been reborn in Baptism.
Through that anointing,
you transform them into the likeness of your Son
and give them a share in his royal, priestly and
    prophetic work.

And so, Father, by the power of your love,
make this mixture of oil and perfume
a sign and source of your blessing.
Pour out the gifts of your Holy Spirit
on our brothers and sisters who will be anointed with it.
Let the splendour of holiness shine on the world
from every place and thing signed with this oil.

Coming to Mass: Bearing Witness to Christ

What is the most important way that we bear witness to Christ, as people anointed to proclaim the Good News to the world? By coming to Mass together! Our willingness to come to church every Sunday and take a full part in the Mass; our willingness to tell our friends and families that Mass is a vital part of Sunday as the Lord's Day; our readiness to change our plans and inconvenience ourselves to make sure we can get to Mass: all of this can speak powerfully of our commitment to Christ. Being part of a community gathered in worship gives us a special strength in our witness. We are not alone. We are each a vital and essential part of something bigger than ourselves. Together, we are the Body of Christ in the world. When we stand together to hear the Gospel of Christ; when we stand to profess our faith in the 'Creed', making our personal faith part of the 'We believe' of the Church; when we come forward with everyone else to receive the Body and Blood of Christ: in each of these ways, and many others, we make public our faith in Jesus and we proclaim him to the world.

'Go in Peace to Love and Serve the Lord'

At the end of Mass, we are blessed and dismissed! Or rather, blessed and 'missioned', commissioned by the Lord! There is perhaps no better summary of what it means to be a confirmed Catholic leaving Sunday Mass than that of the Second Vatican Council: each one of us 'must stand before the world as a witness to the resurrection and life of the Lord Jesus, and as a sign that God lives' (*Lumen Gentium,* no. 38). How's that for a challenge!

When we hear that challenge, we can feel deeply unworthy, too weak to respond. But God does something silently powerful in the sacrament of Confirmation. Whatever we feel on the day, we receive the invisible Gift of the Holy Spirit, the living strength of God himself. God's power shines through our human weakness! The same can be said to God our all-powerful Father about us as we say to him of the martyrs: 'You choose the weak and make them strong in bearing witness to you, through Jesus Christ our Lord.'[15] God gives us a courage far beyond our human limitations. Confirmation is above all something that God does to us, not something that we do for God! His powerful presence makes all the difference deep inside us. St Paul's great prayer to the Father for the Christians in Ephesus is especially appropriate for people preparing to be confirmed or seeking to renew the grace of their Confirmation:

I pray that, according to the riches of his glory,
he may grant that you may be strengthened in your
    inner being
with power through his Spirit,

and that Christ may dwell in your hearts through faith,
as you are being rooted and grounded in love.
I pray that you may have the power to comprehend,
with all the saints,
what is the breadth and length and height and depth,
and to know the love of Christ that surpasses knowledge,
so that you may be filled with all the fullness of God.
Now to him who by the power at work within us
is able to accomplish abundantly far more than all we
    can ask or imagine,
to him be glory in the Church and in Christ Jesus
to all generations, forever and ever.
Amen. (*Eph* 4:16-21)

We are called to be more than an Easter People, gathered
in loving communion with the Risen Lord; we are to be a
Pentecost People, anointed and enflamed by the Holy
Spirit to go out and spread the Good News of salvation.
As Pope John Paul reminded the candidates he was about
to confirm at Coventry in 1982, we are to be 'the people
of Pentecost, the apostles of our time.'

A Prayer For All

Generous God, touch us again with the fire of your Spirit
and renew us by your grace, that we may profess the one
true faith and live in love and unity with all who follow
Christ. Amen.[16]

SOME KEY WORDS

Anoint
A ritual with oil, often showing that a person has been set aside for some special service to God in the Church.

Bishop
A bishop is a successor of the original apostles, and leads, teaches and shepherds a diocese in Christ's name. Every parish is part of a wider diocese.

Chrism
A sacred perfumed oil, often a mixture of olive oil and balsam, used to consecrate special things and people in the Church. Only a bishop can make chrism.

Council (e.g. Trent, Vatican II)
Every now and then, all the bishops of the Catholic Church gather together for a special 'ecumenical' council. What they solemnly teach is kept free from error by the Holy Spirit. The Council of Trent met from 1545-1563. The Second Vatican Council met from 1962-1965.

Eucharist

An ancient name for the Mass. The word comes from the Greek for 'to give thanks'. We come to Mass to lift up our hearts to God, simply because 'it is right to give him thanks and praise.'

Evangelise, evangelisation

These words are rooted in the Greek and Latin words for 'Good News', the Gospel. Proclaiming and spreading the Good News of Jesus Christ is the heart of the Church's life and work.

Initiation

Our gradual welcome into the mystery of Christ in the life of the Church, through being baptised, confirmed and receiving Holy Communion for the first time.

Liturgy

The public worship of the Church.

Pentecost

A Jewish festival which falls on the 50th day after Passover. Christians use the name, above all, for the day when the Holy Spirit came on the Apostles. It is also called 'Whitsun' or 'Whit Sunday', from 'white Sunday', because Baptisms often took place on this feast, with those being baptised wearing white robes.

Sacrament

A visible sign that makes present for us the invisible presence and action of the Risen Jesus. Our Lord touches our lives through the sacraments.

Seal

Originally wax or some other material attached to a document and stamped with a symbol to show it was genuine. At our Baptism and Confirmation, God seals us with his Holy Spirit, as a permanent mark that we belong to him and have a special place and responsibility in the Church.

Sponsor

Someone chosen to accompany and support you at your Confirmation and from then on. He or she should be a confirmed, practising Catholic, at least 16 years old. Ideally, it should be one of your Baptismal godparents.

Vocation

A call from God to serve him in some special way.

END NOTES

[1] Sacred Congregation for Divine Worship, *Introduction to the Rite of Confirmation*, n. 7; *CCC*, n. 1313

[2] St Cyril of Jerusalem (c.AD 350), *Catechesis* 3:2-7

[3] *CCC*, n. 1311.

[4] Pope Paul VI, *Apostolic Constitution on the Sacrament of Confirmation;* cf. *CCC*, n. 1320.

[5] *Catechism of the Catholic Church*, n. 1285.

[6] Catholic Bishops of England and Wales, Ireland, and Scotland; *One Bread, One Body*, 1998; no. 15.

[7] Second Vatican Council, *Lumen Gentium*, no. 11.

[8] From a 3rd century Syrian document, *The Didascalia*

[9] Pope Paul VI

[10] Pope Paul VI, *Apostolic Constitution on the Sacrament of Confirmation* (1971); cf. *CCC*, no. 1288.

[11] Pope Paul VI, *Evangelii Nuntiandi*, no.15.

[12] Catholic Bishops of England and Wales, Ireland, and Scotland; *One Bread, One Body* (1998), no. 66.

[13] *Preface of the Apostles II*

[14] *Preface of Holy Men and Women II*

[15] *Preface of Martyrs*

[16] A prayer from the Confirmation Service in the *Methodist Worship Book* (1999)